THE EXODUS

Exodus 3:1–15:3 for children

Written by Craig John Lovik
Illustrated by Arthur W. Kirchhoff

ARCH BOOKS

Copyright © 1987 Concordia Publishing House
3558 S. Jefferson Avenue, St. Louis, MO   63118-3968
Manufactured in the United States of America

My name is Rehabiah, but
    my friends all call me Rey;
You probably haven't heard of me
    at least until today.
I have a famous Grampa
    (one I'm positive you know):
he told the mighty king of Egypt,
    "Let My people go!"

The trouble all got started when
    the king said, "Something's wrong;
I'm worried that these Hebrew folks
    are getting way too strong.
Something must be done," he groaned,
    "to put this to a stop."
Then with an evil grin he said,
    "We'll work them 'til they drop."

And when the pain and suffering
    was more than folks could stand,
God had a talk with Grampa and
    He told him what He'd planned:
"Please tell that king," said Yahweh,
    "to let My people go.
And, if he will not listen,
    Awesome wonders I will show."

Grampa first protested, but
    he finally did agree
to tell the Pharaoh (Egypt's king):
    "God's people must be free."
Great-uncle Aaron went with Grampa
    to the palace court,
and this is what the Pharaoh said
    to what they did report:
"I will not let these people go;
    your God does not scare me.
Instead, I'll work them harder,
    and I'll never let them free!"
And just as God had promised,
    mighty wonders were in store:
plagues that were so awful that
    the king would beg, "No more!"

God turned the water into blood;
    He filled the land with frogs:
crawling gnats were everywhere
    on people, cats, and dogs.
Each time God sent another plague
    (an awful, deadly sign),
The king of Egypt would repent
    but then would change his mind.
God said, "A final plague will come,
    and then you will be free
to leave this land of Egypt and
    to come and follow Me.
Prepare a lamb, without a spot,
    to eat—don't leave a drop!
Paint its blood upon your doorposts
    and across the top.
And when God's angel sees the blood,
    then he will pass you by;
but for the others in the land,
    the firstborn all will die."

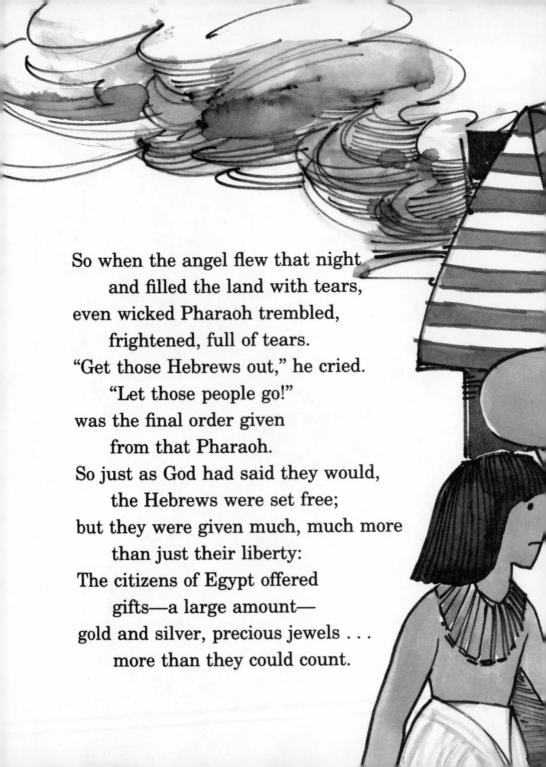

So when the angel flew that night
    and filled the land with tears,
even wicked Pharaoh trembled,
    frightened, full of tears.
"Get those Hebrews out," he cried.
    "Let those people go!"
was the final order given
    from that Pharaoh.
So just as God had said they would,
    the Hebrews were set free;
but they were given much, much more
    than just their liberty:
The citizens of Egypt offered
    gifts—a large amount—
gold and silver, precious jewels . . .
    more than they could count.

God led them out of Egypt,
        bound for Canaan to be free;
but rather than on easy road,
        He led them to a sea.
He showed that He was present
        by a cloudy pillar bright
which changed its form to fiery pillar,
        leading them by night.

The Pharaoh changed his mind and sent
        his soldiers after them
to get the sons of Israel
        and make them slaves again.
The people ran! The soldiers came
        in chariots, angrily!
The people kept on running 'til
        they ran against the sea.
"What have you done?"
        they asked my Grampa,
        seeing soldiers near;
"better to be slaves in Egypt
        than to die out here!"

My Grampa prayed to God, and God
      was quick to hear his plea:
"Lift up your walking stick and hold it
      out above the sea.
The sea will split as I see fit,
      and you can cross it dry;
I'll guard you with My cloudy pillar!"
      This was God's reply.
God opened up the mighty sea
      so they could march across,
escaping Egypt's army, which
      then suffered total loss.
And when they safely gathered 'cross
      upon the other bank,
Gramps and all the Hebrews sang
      a happy song of thanks:

"Our God," they sang with all their might,
    "has triumphed gloriously!
The horse and rider of our foes
    He's thrown into the sea.
Our God's a mighty Savior
    and a mighty Man of war.
We'll shout and sing His praises loud
    right now and evermore!"

By now you know my Grampa—
  he who sang about God's fame—
I'm sure that you have guessed by now
  that *Moses* was his name.

DEAR PARENTS:

Now there arose up a new king over Egypt, which knew not Joseph. And he said unto his people, "Behold, the people of the children of Israel are more and mightier than we; . . . Therefore they did set over them taskmasters to afflict them with their burdens."

The story Rehabiah (*ree* huh BIGH uh) tells—the story of the Exodus—is one of rescue, of redemption, the redemption of Israel from enslavement by the Egyptians, who "made their lives bitter with hard labor in brick and mortar and with all kinds of work in the fields; in all their hard labor the Egyptians used them ruthlessly" (Exodus 1:14 NIV).

Israel's redemption is not of its own making. In love, and because they are His own dear people, God responds to the anguish of the Israelites: "I have indeed seen the misery of my people in Egypt," He says to Moses. "So I have come down to rescue them from the hand of the Egyptians and to bring them up out of that land. . . . So now, go. I am sending you to Pharaoh to bring my people the Israelites out of Egypt" (Exodus 2:7a, 8a, 10 NIV).

The story of the Exodus also points to an even greater rescue. Just as God sent Moses to rescue Israel from the grasp of Pharaoh, so He sent His own Son to rescue all of us from the grasp of Satan and eternal death. "It was not with perishable things such as silver or gold that you were redeemed . . . but with the precious blood of Christ, a lamb without blemish or defect" (1 Peter 1:18–19 NIV).

When you share with your child the story of Moses and the Exodus, use the opportunity, too, to tell your child the story of God's greatest rescue, how He sent His own dear Son so that someday we might share in the eternal joy of heaven.

THE EDITOR